MY PURCHASE

Website/store	Item(s) bought
Order ID	
Order date	Paid via
Tracking no	Notes/return info
Date shipped	Date received

MY PURCHASE

Website/store	Item(s) bought
Order ID	
Order date	Paid via
Tracking no	Notes/return info
Date shipped	Date received

MY PURCHASE

Website/store	Item(s) bought
Order ID	
Order date	Paid via
Tracking no	Notes/return info
Date shipped	Date received

MY PURCHASE

Website/store	Item(s) bought
Order ID	
Order date	Paid via
Tracking no	Notes/return info
Date shipped	Date received

MY PURCHASE

Website/store	Item(s) bought
Order ID	
Order date	Paid via
Tracking no	Notes/return info
Date shipped	Date received

MY PURCHASE

Website/store	Item(s) bought
Order ID	
Order date	Paid via
Tracking no	Notes/return info
Date shipped	Date received

MY PURCHASE

Website/store	Item(s) bought
Order ID	
Order date	Paid via
Tracking no	Notes/return info
Date shipped	Date received

MY PURCHASE

Website/store	Item(s) bought
Order ID	
Order date	Paid via
Tracking no	Notes/return info
Date shipped	Date received

MY PURCHASE

Website/store	Item(s) bought
Order ID	
Order date	Paid via
Tracking no	Notes/return info
Date shipped	Date received

MY PURCHASE

Website/store	Item(s) bought
Order ID	
Order date	Paid via
Tracking no	Notes/return info
Date shipped	Date received

MY PURCHASE

Website/store	Item(s) bought
Order ID	
Order date	Paid via
Tracking no	Notes/return info
Date shipped	Date received

MY PURCHASE

Website/store	Item(s) bought
Order ID	
Order date	Paid via
Tracking no	Notes/return info
Date shipped	Date received

MY PURCHASE

Website/store	Item(s) bought
Order ID	
Order date	Paid via
Tracking no	Notes/return info
Date shipped	Date received

MY PURCHASE

Website/store	Item(s) bought
Order ID	
Order date	Paid via
Tracking no	Notes/return info
Date shipped	Date received

MY PURCHASE

Website/store	Item(s) bought
Order ID	
Order date	Paid via
Tracking no	Notes/return info
Date shipped	Date received

MY PURCHASE

Website/store	Item(s) bought
Order ID	
Order date	Paid via
Tracking no	Notes/return info
Date shipped	Date received

MY PURCHASE

Website/store	Item(s) bought
Order ID	
Order date	Paid via
Tracking no	Notes/return info
Date shipped	Date received

MY PURCHASE

Website/store	Item(s) bought
Order ID	
Order date	Paid via
Tracking no	Notes/return info
Date shipped	Date received

My Purchase

Website/store	Item(s) bought
Order ID	
Order date	Paid via
Tracking no	Notes/return info
Date shipped	Date received

My Purchase

Website/store	Item(s) bought
Order ID	
Order date	Paid via
Tracking no	Notes/return info
Date shipped	Date received

My Purchase

Website/store	Item(s) bought
Order ID	
Order date	Paid via
Tracking no	Notes/return info
Date shipped	Date received

MY PURCHASE

Website/store	Item(s) bought
Order ID	
Order date	Paid via
Tracking no	Notes/return info
Date shipped	Date received

MY PURCHASE

Website/store	Item(s) bought
Order ID	
Order date	Paid via
Tracking no	Notes/return info
Date shipped	Date received

MY PURCHASE

Website/store	Item(s) bought
Order ID	
Order date	Paid via
Tracking no	Notes/return info
Date shipped	Date received

MY PURCHASE

Website/store	Item(s) bought
Order ID	
Order date	Paid via
Tracking no	Notes/return info
Date shipped	Date received

MY PURCHASE

Website/store	Item(s) bought
Order ID	
Order date	Paid via
Tracking no	Notes/return info
Date shipped	Date received

MY PURCHASE

Website/store	Item(s) bought
Order ID	
Order date	Paid via
Tracking no	Notes/return info
Date shipped	Date received

MY PURCHASE

Website/store	Item(s) bought
Order ID	
Order date	Paid via
Tracking no	Notes/return info
Date shipped	Date received

MY PURCHASE

Website/store	Item(s) bought
Order ID	
Order date	Paid via
Tracking no	Notes/return info
Date shipped	Date received

MY PURCHASE

Website/store	Item(s) bought
Order ID	
Order date	Paid via
Tracking no	Notes/return info
Date shipped	Date received

MY PURCHASE

Website/store	Item(s) bought
Order ID	
Order date	Paid via
Tracking no	Notes/return info
Date shipped	Date received

MY PURCHASE

Website/store	Item(s) bought
Order ID	
Order date	Paid via
Tracking no	Notes/return info
Date shipped	Date received

MY PURCHASE

Website/store	Item(s) bought
Order ID	
Order date	Paid via
Tracking no	Notes/return info
Date shipped	Date received

MY PURCHASE

Website/store	Item(s) bought
Order ID	
Order date	Paid via
Tracking no	Notes/return info
Date shipped	Date received

MY PURCHASE

Website/store	Item(s) bought
Order ID	
Order date	Paid via
Tracking no	Notes/return info
Date shipped	Date received

MY PURCHASE

Website/store	Item(s) bought
Order ID	
Order date	Paid via
Tracking no	Notes/return info
Date shipped	Date received

MY PURCHASE

Website/store	Item(s) bought
Order ID	
Order date	Paid via
Tracking no	Notes/return info
Date shipped	Date received

MY PURCHASE

Website/store	Item(s) bought
Order ID	
Order date	Paid via
Tracking no	Notes/return info
Date shipped	Date received

MY PURCHASE

Website/store	Item(s) bought
Order ID	
Order date	Paid via
Tracking no	Notes/return info
Date shipped	Date received

MY PURCHASE

Website/store	Item(s) bought
Order ID	
Order date	Paid via
Tracking no	Notes/return info
Date shipped	Date received

MY PURCHASE

Website/store	Item(s) bought
Order ID	
Order date	Paid via
Tracking no	Notes/return info
Date shipped	Date received

MY PURCHASE

Website/store	Item(s) bought
Order ID	
Order date	Paid via
Tracking no	Notes/return info
Date shipped	Date received

MY PURCHASE

Website/store	Item(s) bought
Order ID	
Order date	Paid via
Tracking no	Notes/return info
Date shipped	Date received

MY PURCHASE

Website/store	Item(s) bought
Order ID	
Order date	Paid via
Tracking no	Notes/return info
Date shipped	Date received

MY PURCHASE

Website/store	Item(s) bought
Order ID	
Order date	Paid via
Tracking no	Notes/return info
Date shipped	Date received

MY PURCHASE

Website/store	Item(s) bought
Order ID	
Order date	Paid via
Tracking no	Notes/return info
Date shipped	Date received

MY PURCHASE

Website/store	Item(s) bought
Order ID	
Order date	Paid via
Tracking no	Notes/return info
Date shipped	Date received

MY PURCHASE

Website/store	Item(s) bought
Order ID	
Order date	Paid via
Tracking no	Notes/return info
Date shipped	Date received

MY PURCHASE

Website/store	Item(s) bought
Order ID	
Order date	Paid via
Tracking no	Notes/return info
Date shipped	Date received

MY PURCHASE

Website/store	Item(s) bought
Order ID	
Order date	Paid via
Tracking no	Notes/return info
Date shipped	Date received

MY PURCHASE

Website/store	Item(s) bought
Order ID	
Order date	Paid via
Tracking no	Notes/return info
Date shipped	Date received

MY PURCHASE

Website/store	Item(s) bought
Order ID	
Order date	Paid via
Tracking no	Notes/return info
Date shipped	Date received

MY PURCHASE

Website/store	Item(s) bought
Order ID	
Order date	Paid via
Tracking no	Notes/return info
Date shipped	Date received

MY PURCHASE

Website/store	Item(s) bought
Order ID	
Order date	Paid via
Tracking no	Notes/return info
Date shipped	Date received

MY PURCHASE

Website/store	Item(s) bought
Order ID	
Order date	Paid via
Tracking no	Notes/return info
Date shipped	Date received

MY PURCHASE

Website/store	Item(s) bought
Order ID	
Order date	Paid via
Tracking no	Notes/return info
Date shipped	Date received

MY PURCHASE

Website/store	Item(s) bought
Order ID	
Order date	Paid via
Tracking no	Notes/return info
Date shipped	Date received

MY PURCHASE

Website/store	Item(s) bought
Order ID	
Order date	Paid via
Tracking no	Notes/return info
Date shipped	Date received

MY PURCHASE

Website/store	Item(s) bought
Order ID	
Order date	Paid via
Tracking no	Notes/return info
Date shipped	Date received

MY PURCHASE

Website/store	Item(s) bought
Order ID	
Order date	Paid via
Tracking no	Notes/return info
Date shipped	Date received

MY PURCHASE

Website/store	Item(s) bought
Order ID	
Order date	Paid via
Tracking no	Notes/return info
Date shipped	Date received

MY PURCHASE

Website/store	Item(s) bought
Order ID	
Order date	Paid via
Tracking no	Notes/return info
Date shipped	Date received

MY PURCHASE

Website/store	Item(s) bought
Order ID	
Order date	Paid via
Tracking no	Notes/return info
Date shipped	Date received

MY PURCHASE

Website/store	Item(s) bought
Order ID	
Order date	Paid via
Tracking no	Notes/return info
Date shipped	Date received

MY PURCHASE

Website/store	Item(s) bought
Order ID	
Order date	Paid via
Tracking no	Notes/return info
Date shipped	Date received

MY PURCHASE

Website/store	Item(s) bought
Order ID	
Order date	Paid via
Tracking no	Notes/return info
Date shipped	Date received

MY PURCHASE

Website/store	Item(s) bought
Order ID	
Order date	Paid via
Tracking no	Notes/return info
Date shipped	Date received

MY PURCHASE

Website/store	Item(s) bought
Order ID	
Order date	Paid via
Tracking no	Notes/return info
Date shipped	Date received

MY PURCHASE

Website/store	Item(s) bought
Order ID	
Order date	Paid via
Tracking no	Notes/return info
Date shipped	Date received

MY PURCHASE

Website/store	Item(s) bought
Order ID	
Order date	Paid via
Tracking no	Notes/return info
Date shipped	Date received

MY PURCHASE

Website/store	Item(s) bought
Order ID	
Order date	Paid via
Tracking no	Notes/return info
Date shipped	Date received

MY PURCHASE

Website/store	Item(s) bought
Order ID	
Order date	Paid via
Tracking no	Notes/return info
Date shipped	Date received

MY PURCHASE

Website/store	Item(s) bought
Order ID	
Order date	Paid via
Tracking no	Notes/return info
Date shipped	Date received

MY PURCHASE

Website/store	Item(s) bought
Order ID	
Order date	Paid via
Tracking no	Notes/return info
Date shipped	Date received

MY PURCHASE

Website/store	Item(s) bought
Order ID	
Order date	Paid via
Tracking no	Notes/return info
Date shipped	Date received

MY PURCHASE

Website/store	Item(s) bought
Order ID	
Order date	Paid via
Tracking no	Notes/return info
Date shipped	Date received

MY PURCHASE

Website/store	Item(s) bought
Order ID	
Order date	Paid via
Tracking no	Notes/return info
Date shipped	Date received

MY PURCHASE

Website/store	Item(s) bought
Order ID	
Order date	Paid via
Tracking no	Notes/return info
Date shipped	Date received

MY PURCHASE

Website/store	Item(s) bought
Order ID	
Order date	Paid via
Tracking no	Notes/return info
Date shipped	Date received

MY PURCHASE

Website/store	Item(s) bought
Order ID	
Order date	Paid via
Tracking no	Notes/return info
Date shipped	Date received

MY PURCHASE

Website/store	Item(s) bought
Order ID	
Order date	Paid via
Tracking no	Notes/return info
Date shipped	Date received

MY PURCHASE

Website/store	Item(s) bought
Order ID	
Order date	Paid via
Tracking no	Notes/return info
Date shipped	Date received

MY PURCHASE

Website/store	Item(s) bought
Order ID	
Order date	Paid via
Tracking no	Notes/return info
Date shipped	Date received

MY PURCHASE

Website/store	Item(s) bought
Order ID	
Order date	Paid via
Tracking no	Notes/return info
Date shipped	Date received

MY PURCHASE

Website/store	Item(s) bought
Order ID	
Order date	Paid via
Tracking no	Notes/return info
Date shipped	Date received

MY PURCHASE

Website/store	Item(s) bought
Order ID	
Order date	Paid via
Tracking no	Notes/return info
Date shipped	Date received

MY PURCHASE

Website/store	Item(s) bought
Order ID	
Order date	Paid via
Tracking no	Notes/return info
Date shipped	Date received

MY PURCHASE

Website/store	Item(s) bought
Order ID	
Order date	Paid via
Tracking no	Notes/return info
Date shipped	Date received

MY PURCHASE

Website/store	Item(s) bought
Order ID	
Order date	Paid via
Tracking no	Notes/return info
Date shipped	Date received

MY PURCHASE

Website/store	Item(s) bought
Order ID	
Order date	Paid via
Tracking no	Notes/return info
Date shipped	Date received

MY PURCHASE

Website/store	Item(s) bought
Order ID	
Order date	Paid via
Tracking no	Notes/return info
Date shipped	Date received

MY PURCHASE

Website/store	Item(s) bought
Order ID	
Order date	Paid via
Tracking no	Notes/return info
Date shipped	Date received

MY PURCHASE

Website/store	Item(s) bought
Order ID	
Order date	Paid via
Tracking no	Notes/return info
Date shipped	Date received

MY PURCHASE

Website/store	Item(s) bought
Order ID	
Order date	Paid via
Tracking no	Notes/return info
Date shipped	Date received

MY PURCHASE

Website/store	Item(s) bought
Order ID	
Order date	Paid via
Tracking no	Notes/return info
Date shipped	Date received

MY PURCHASE

Website/store	Item(s) bought
Order ID	
Order date	Paid via
Tracking no	Notes/return info
Date shipped	Date received

MY PURCHASE

Website/store	Item(s) bought
Order ID	
Order date	Paid via
Tracking no	Notes/return info
Date shipped	Date received

MY PURCHASE

Website/store	Item(s) bought
Order ID	
Order date	Paid via
Tracking no	Notes/return info
Date shipped	Date received

MY PURCHASE

Website/store	Item(s) bought
Order ID	
Order date	Paid via
Tracking no	Notes/return info
Date shipped	Date received

MY PURCHASE

Website/store	Item(s) bought
Order ID	
Order date	Paid via
Tracking no	Notes/return info
Date shipped	Date received

MY PURCHASE

Website/store	Item(s) bought
Order ID	
Order date	Paid via
Tracking no	Notes/return info
Date shipped	Date received

MY PURCHASE

Website/store	Item(s) bought
Order ID	
Order date	Paid via
Tracking no	Notes/return info
Date shipped	Date received

MY PURCHASE

Website/store	Item(s) bought
Order ID	
Order date	Paid via
Tracking no	Notes/return info
Date shipped	Date received

MY PURCHASE

Website/store	Item(s) bought
Order ID	
Order date	Paid via
Tracking no	Notes/return info
Date shipped	Date received

MY PURCHASE

Website/store	Item(s) bought
Order ID	
Order date	Paid via
Tracking no	Notes/return info
Date shipped	Date received

MY PURCHASE

Website/store	Item(s) bought
Order ID	
Order date	Paid via
Tracking no	Notes/return info
Date shipped	Date received

MY PURCHASE

Website/store	Item(s) bought
Order ID	
Order date	Paid via
Tracking no	Notes/return info
Date shipped	Date received

MY PURCHASE

Website/store	Item(s) bought
Order ID	
Order date	Paid via
Tracking no	Notes/return info
Date shipped	Date received

MY PURCHASE

Website/store	Item(s) bought
Order ID	
Order date	Paid via
Tracking no	Notes/return info
Date shipped	Date received

MY PURCHASE

Website/store	Item(s) bought
Order ID	
Order date	Paid via
Tracking no	Notes/return info
Date shipped	Date received

MY PURCHASE

Website/store	Item(s) bought
Order ID	
Order date	Paid via
Tracking no	Notes/return info
Date shipped	Date received

MY PURCHASE

Website/store	Item(s) bought
Order ID	
Order date	Paid via
Tracking no	Notes/return info
Date shipped	Date received

MY PURCHASE

Website/store	Item(s) bought
Order ID	
Order date	Paid via
Tracking no	Notes/return info
Date shipped	Date received

MY PURCHASE

Website/store	Item(s) bought
Order ID	
Order date	Paid via
Tracking no	Notes/return info
Date shipped	Date received

MY PURCHASE

Website/store	Item(s) bought
Order ID	
Order date	Paid via
Tracking no	Notes/return info
Date shipped	Date received

MY PURCHASE

Website/store	Item(s) bought
Order ID	
Order date	Paid via
Tracking no	Notes/return info
Date shipped	Date received

MY PURCHASE

Website/store	Item(s) bought
Order ID	
Order date	Paid via
Tracking no	Notes/return info
Date shipped	Date received

MY PURCHASE

Website/store	Item(s) bought
Order ID	
Order date	Paid via
Tracking no	Notes/return info
Date shipped	Date received

MY PURCHASE

Website/store	Item(s) bought
Order ID	
Order date	Paid via
Tracking no	Notes/return info
Date shipped	Date received

MY PURCHASE

Website/store	Item(s) bought
Order ID	
Order date	Paid via
Tracking no	Notes/return info
Date shipped	Date received

MY PURCHASE

Website/store	Item(s) bought
Order ID	
Order date	Paid via
Tracking no	Notes/return info
Date shipped	Date received

MY PURCHASE

Website/store	Item(s) bought
Order ID	
Order date	Paid via
Tracking no	Notes/return info
Date shipped	Date received

MY PURCHASE

Website/store	Item(s) bought
Order ID	
Order date	Paid via
Tracking no	Notes/return info
Date shipped	Date received

MY PURCHASE

Website/store	Item(s) bought
Order ID	
Order date	Paid via
Tracking no	Notes/return info
Date shipped	Date received

MY PURCHASE

Website/store	Item(s) bought
Order ID	
Order date	Paid via
Tracking no	Notes/return info
Date shipped	Date received

MY PURCHASE

Website/store	Item(s) bought
Order ID	
Order date	Paid via
Tracking no	Notes/return info
Date shipped	Date received

MY PURCHASE

Website/store	Item(s) bought
Order ID	
Order date	Paid via
Tracking no	Notes/return info
Date shipped	Date received

MY PURCHASE

Website/store	Item(s) bought
Order ID	
Order date	Paid via
Tracking no	Notes/return info
Date shipped	Date received

MY PURCHASE

Website/store	Item(s) bought
Order ID	
Order date	Paid via
Tracking no	Notes/return info
Date shipped	Date received

MY PURCHASE

Website/store	Item(s) bought
Order ID	
Order date	Paid via
Tracking no	Notes/return info
Date shipped	Date received

MY PURCHASE

Website/store	Item(s) bought
Order ID	
Order date	Paid via
Tracking no	Notes/return info
Date shipped	Date received

MY PURCHASE

Website/store	Item(s) bought
Order ID	
Order date	Paid via
Tracking no	Notes/return info
Date shipped	Date received

MY PURCHASE

Website/store	Item(s) bought
Order ID	
Order date	Paid via
Tracking no	Notes/return info
Date shipped	Date received

MY PURCHASE

Website/store	Item(s) bought
Order ID	
Order date	Paid via
Tracking no	Notes/return info
Date shipped	Date received

MY PURCHASE

Website/store	Item(s) bought
Order ID	
Order date	Paid via
Tracking no	Notes/return info
Date shipped	Date received

MY PURCHASE

Website/store	Item(s) bought
Order ID	
Order date	Paid via
Tracking no	Notes/return info
Date shipped	Date received

MY PURCHASE

Website/store	Item(s) bought
Order ID	
Order date	Paid via
Tracking no	Notes/return info
Date shipped	Date received

MY PURCHASE

Website/store	Item(s) bought
Order ID	
Order date	Paid via
Tracking no	Notes/return info
Date shipped	Date received

MY PURCHASE

Website/store	Item(s) bought
Order ID	
Order date	Paid via
Tracking no	Notes/return info
Date shipped	Date received

MY PURCHASE

Website/store	Item(s) bought
Order ID	
Order date	Paid via
Tracking no	Notes/return info
Date shipped	Date received

MY PURCHASE

Website/store	Item(s) bought
Order ID	
Order date	Paid via
Tracking no	Notes/return info
Date shipped	Date received

MY PURCHASE

Website/store	Item(s) bought
Order ID	
Order date	Paid via
Tracking no	Notes/return info
Date shipped	Date received

MY PURCHASE

Website/store	Item(s) bought
Order ID	
Order date	Paid via
Tracking no	Notes/return info
Date shipped	Date received

MY PURCHASE

Website/store	Item(s) bought
Order ID	
Order date	Paid via
Tracking no	Notes/return info
Date shipped	Date received

MY PURCHASE

Website/store	Item(s) bought
Order ID	
Order date	Paid via
Tracking no	Notes/return info
Date shipped	Date received

MY PURCHASE

Website/store	Item(s) bought
Order ID	
Order date	Paid via
Tracking no	Notes/return info
Date shipped	Date received

MY PURCHASE

Website/store	Item(s) bought
Order ID	
Order date	Paid via
Tracking no	Notes/return info
Date shipped	Date received

MY PURCHASE

Website/store	Item(s) bought
Order ID	
Order date	Paid via
Tracking no	Notes/return info
Date shipped	Date received

MY PURCHASE

Website/store	Item(s) bought
Order ID	
Order date	Paid via
Tracking no	Notes/return info
Date shipped	Date received

MY PURCHASE

Website/store	Item(s) bought
Order ID	
Order date	Paid via
Tracking no	Notes/return info
Date shipped	Date received

MY PURCHASE

Website/store	Item(s) bought
Order ID	
Order date	Paid via
Tracking no	Notes/return info
Date shipped	Date received

MY PURCHASE

Website/store	Item(s) bought
Order ID	
Order date	Paid via
Tracking no	Notes/return info
Date shipped	Date received

MY PURCHASE

Website/store	Item(s) bought
Order ID	
Order date	Paid via
Tracking no	Notes/return info
Date shipped	Date received

MY PURCHASE

Website/store	Item(s) bought
Order ID	
Order date	Paid via
Tracking no	Notes/return info
Date shipped	Date received

MY PURCHASE

Website/store	Item(s) bought
Order ID	
Order date	Paid via
Tracking no	Notes/return info
Date shipped	Date received

MY PURCHASE

Website/store	Item(s) bought
Order ID	
Order date	Paid via
Tracking no	Notes/return info
Date shipped	Date received

MY PURCHASE

Website/store	Item(s) bought
Order ID	
Order date	Paid via
Tracking no	Notes/return info
Date shipped	Date received

MY PURCHASE

Website/store	Item(s) bought
Order ID	
Order date	Paid via
Tracking no	Notes/return info
Date shipped	Date received

MY PURCHASE

Website/store	Item(s) bought
Order ID	
Order date	Paid via
Tracking no	Notes/return info
Date shipped	Date received

MY PURCHASE

Website/store	Item(s) bought
Order ID	
Order date	Paid via
Tracking no	Notes/return info
Date shipped	Date received

MY PURCHASE

Website/store	Item(s) bought
Order ID	
Order date	Paid via
Tracking no	Notes/return info
Date shipped	Date received

MY PURCHASE

Website/store	Item(s) bought
Order ID	
Order date	Paid via
Tracking no	Notes/return info
Date shipped	Date received

MY PURCHASE

Website/store	Item(s) bought
Order ID	
Order date	Paid via
Tracking no	Notes/return info
Date shipped	Date received

MY PURCHASE

Website/store	Item(s) bought
Order ID	
Order date	Paid via
Tracking no	Notes/return info
Date shipped	Date received

MY PURCHASE

Website/store	Item(s) bought
Order ID	
Order date	Paid via
Tracking no	Notes/return info
Date shipped	Date received

MY PURCHASE

Website/store	Item(s) bought
Order ID	
Order date	Paid via
Tracking no	Notes/return info
Date shipped	Date received

MY PURCHASE

Website/store	Item(s) bought
Order ID	
Order date	Paid via
Tracking no	Notes/return info
Date shipped	Date received

MY PURCHASE

Website/store	Item(s) bought
Order ID	
Order date	Paid via
Tracking no	Notes/return info
Date shipped	Date received

MY PURCHASE

Website/store	Item(s) bought
Order ID	
Order date	Paid via
Tracking no	Notes/return info
Date shipped	Date received

MY PURCHASE

Website/store	Item(s) bought
Order ID	
Order date	Paid via
Tracking no	Notes/return info
Date shipped	Date received

MY PURCHASE

Website/store	Item(s) bought
Order ID	
Order date	Paid via
Tracking no	Notes/return info
Date shipped	Date received

MY PURCHASE

Website/store	Item(s) bought
Order ID	
Order date	Paid via
Tracking no	Notes/return info
Date shipped	Date received

MY PURCHASE

Website/store	Item(s) bought
Order ID	
Order date	Paid via
Tracking no	Notes/return info
Date shipped	Date received

MY PURCHASE

Website/store	Item(s) bought
Order ID	
Order date	Paid via
Tracking no	Notes/return info
Date shipped	Date received

MY PURCHASE

Website/store	Item(s) bought
Order ID	
Order date	Paid via
Tracking no	Notes/return info
Date shipped	Date received

MY PURCHASE

Website/store	Item(s) bought
Order ID	
Order date	Paid via
Tracking no	Notes/return info
Date shipped	Date received

MY PURCHASE

Website/store	Item(s) bought
Order ID	
Order date	Paid via
Tracking no	Notes/return info
Date shipped	Date received

MY PURCHASE

Website/store	Item(s) bought
Order ID	
Order date	Paid via
Tracking no	Notes/return info
Date shipped	Date received

MY PURCHASE

Website/store	Item(s) bought
Order ID	
Order date	Paid via
Tracking no	Notes/return info
Date shipped	Date received

MY PURCHASE

Website/store	Item(s) bought
Order ID	
Order date	Paid via
Tracking no	Notes/return info
Date shipped	Date received

My Purchase

Website/store	Item(s) bought
Order ID	
Order date	Paid via
Tracking no	Notes/return info
Date shipped	Date received

My Purchase

Website/store	Item(s) bought
Order ID	
Order date	Paid via
Tracking no	Notes/return info
Date shipped	Date received

My Purchase

Website/store	Item(s) bought
Order ID	
Order date	Paid via
Tracking no	Notes/return info
Date shipped	Date received

MY PURCHASE

Website/store	Item(s) bought
Order ID	
Order date	Paid via
Tracking no	Notes/return info
Date shipped	Date received

MY PURCHASE

Website/store	Item(s) bought
Order ID	
Order date	Paid via
Tracking no	Notes/return info
Date shipped	Date received

MY PURCHASE

Website/store	Item(s) bought
Order ID	
Order date	Paid via
Tracking no	Notes/return info
Date shipped	Date received

MY PURCHASE

Website/store	Item(s) bought
Order ID	
Order date	Paid via
Tracking no	Notes/return info
Date shipped	Date received

MY PURCHASE

Website/store	Item(s) bought
Order ID	
Order date	Paid via
Tracking no	Notes/return info
Date shipped	Date received

MY PURCHASE

Website/store	Item(s) bought
Order ID	
Order date	Paid via
Tracking no	Notes/return info
Date shipped	Date received

MY PURCHASE

Website/store	Item(s) bought
Order ID	
Order date	Paid via
Tracking no	Notes/return info
Date shipped	Date received

MY PURCHASE

Website/store	Item(s) bought
Order ID	
Order date	Paid via
Tracking no	Notes/return info
Date shipped	Date received

MY PURCHASE

Website/store	Item(s) bought
Order ID	
Order date	Paid via
Tracking no	Notes/return info
Date shipped	Date received

MY PURCHASE

Website/store	Item(s) bought
Order ID	
Order date	Paid via
Tracking no	Notes/return info
Date shipped	Date received

MY PURCHASE

Website/store	Item(s) bought
Order ID	
Order date	Paid via
Tracking no	Notes/return info
Date shipped	Date received

MY PURCHASE

Website/store	Item(s) bought
Order ID	
Order date	Paid via
Tracking no	Notes/return info
Date shipped	Date received

MY PURCHASE

Website/store	Item(s) bought
Order ID	
Order date	Paid via
Tracking no	Notes/return info
Date shipped	Date received

MY PURCHASE

Website/store	Item(s) bought
Order ID	
Order date	Paid via
Tracking no	Notes/return info
Date shipped	Date received

MY PURCHASE

Website/store	Item(s) bought
Order ID	
Order date	Paid via
Tracking no	Notes/return info
Date shipped	Date received

MY PURCHASE

Website/store	Item(s) bought
Order ID	
Order date	Paid via
Tracking no	Notes/return info
Date shipped	Date received

MY PURCHASE

Website/store	Item(s) bought
Order ID	
Order date	Paid via
Tracking no	Notes/return info
Date shipped	Date received

MY PURCHASE

Website/store	Item(s) bought
Order ID	
Order date	Paid via
Tracking no	Notes/return info
Date shipped	Date received

MY PURCHASE

Website/store	Item(s) bought
Order ID	
Order date	Paid via
Tracking no	Notes/return info
Date shipped	Date received

MY PURCHASE

Website/store	Item(s) bought
Order ID	
Order date	Paid via
Tracking no	Notes/return info
Date shipped	Date received

MY PURCHASE

Website/store	Item(s) bought
Order ID	
Order date	Paid via
Tracking no	Notes/return info
Date shipped	Date received

MY PURCHASE

Website/store	Item(s) bought
Order ID	
Order date	Paid via
Tracking no	Notes/return info
Date shipped	Date received

MY PURCHASE

Website/store	Item(s) bought
Order ID	
Order date	Paid via
Tracking no	Notes/return info
Date shipped	Date received

MY PURCHASE

Website/store	Item(s) bought
Order ID	
Order date	Paid via
Tracking no	Notes/return info
Date shipped	Date received

MY PURCHASE

Website/store	Item(s) bought
Order ID	
Order date	Paid via
Tracking no	Notes/return info
Date shipped	Date received

MY PURCHASE

Website/store	Item(s) bought
Order ID	
Order date	Paid via
Tracking no	Notes/return info
Date shipped	Date received

MY PURCHASE

Website/store	Item(s) bought
Order ID	
Order date	Paid via
Tracking no	Notes/return info
Date shipped	Date received

MY PURCHASE

Website/store	Item(s) bought
Order ID	
Order date	Paid via
Tracking no	Notes/return info
Date shipped	Date received

MY PURCHASE

Website/store	Item(s) bought
Order ID	
Order date	Paid via
Tracking no	Notes/return info
Date shipped	Date received

MY PURCHASE

Website/store	Item(s) bought
Order ID	
Order date	Paid via
Tracking no	Notes/return info
Date shipped	Date received

MY PURCHASE

Website/store	Item(s) bought
Order ID	
Order date	Paid via
Tracking no	Notes/return info
Date shipped	Date received

MY PURCHASE

Website/store	Item(s) bought
Order ID	
Order date	Paid via
Tracking no	Notes/return info
Date shipped	Date received

MY PURCHASE

Website/store	Item(s) bought
Order ID	
Order date	Paid via
Tracking no	Notes/return info
Date shipped	Date received

My Purchase

Website/store	Item(s) bought
Order ID	
Order date	Paid via
Tracking no	Notes/return info
Date shipped	Date received

My Purchase

Website/store	Item(s) bought
Order ID	
Order date	Paid via
Tracking no	Notes/return info
Date shipped	Date received

My Purchase

Website/store	Item(s) bought
Order ID	
Order date	Paid via
Tracking no	Notes/return info
Date shipped	Date received

MY PURCHASE

Website/store	Item(s) bought
Order ID	
Order date	Paid via
Tracking no	Notes/return info
Date shipped	Date received

MY PURCHASE

Website/store	Item(s) bought
Order ID	
Order date	Paid via
Tracking no	Notes/return info
Date shipped	Date received

MY PURCHASE

Website/store	Item(s) bought
Order ID	
Order date	Paid via
Tracking no	Notes/return info
Date shipped	Date received

MY PURCHASE

Website/store	Item(s) bought
Order ID	
Order date	Paid via
Tracking no	Notes/return info
Date shipped	Date received

MY PURCHASE

Website/store	Item(s) bought
Order ID	
Order date	Paid via
Tracking no	Notes/return info
Date shipped	Date received

MY PURCHASE

Website/store	Item(s) bought
Order ID	
Order date	Paid via
Tracking no	Notes/return info
Date shipped	Date received

MY PURCHASE

Website/store	Item(s) bought
Order ID	
Order date	Paid via
Tracking no	Notes/return info
Date shipped	Date received

MY PURCHASE

Website/store	Item(s) bought
Order ID	
Order date	Paid via
Tracking no	Notes/return info
Date shipped	Date received

MY PURCHASE

Website/store	Item(s) bought
Order ID	
Order date	Paid via
Tracking no	Notes/return info
Date shipped	Date received

MY PURCHASE

Website/store	Item(s) bought
Order ID	
Order date	Paid via
Tracking no	Notes/return info
Date shipped	Date received

MY PURCHASE

Website/store	Item(s) bought
Order ID	
Order date	Paid via
Tracking no	Notes/return info
Date shipped	Date received

MY PURCHASE

Website/store	Item(s) bought
Order ID	
Order date	Paid via
Tracking no	Notes/return info
Date shipped	Date received

MY PURCHASE

Website/store	Item(s) bought
Order ID	
Order date	Paid via
Tracking no	Notes/return info
Date shipped	Date received

MY PURCHASE

Website/store	Item(s) bought
Order ID	
Order date	Paid via
Tracking no	Notes/return info
Date shipped	Date received

MY PURCHASE

Website/store	Item(s) bought
Order ID	
Order date	Paid via
Tracking no	Notes/return info
Date shipped	Date received

MY PURCHASE

Website/store	Item(s) bought
Order ID	
Order date	Paid via
Tracking no	Notes/return info
Date shipped	Date received

MY PURCHASE

Website/store	Item(s) bought
Order ID	
Order date	Paid via
Tracking no	Notes/return info
Date shipped	Date received

MY PURCHASE

Website/store	Item(s) bought
Order ID	
Order date	Paid via
Tracking no	Notes/return info
Date shipped	Date received

MY PURCHASE

Website/store	Item(s) bought
Order ID	
Order date	Paid via
Tracking no	Notes/return info
Date shipped	Date received

MY PURCHASE

Website/store	Item(s) bought
Order ID	
Order date	Paid via
Tracking no	Notes/return info
Date shipped	Date received

MY PURCHASE

Website/store	Item(s) bought
Order ID	
Order date	Paid via
Tracking no	Notes/return info
Date shipped	Date received

MY PURCHASE

Website/store	Item(s) bought
Order ID	
Order date	Paid via
Tracking no	Notes/return info
Date shipped	Date received

MY PURCHASE

Website/store	Item(s) bought
Order ID	
Order date	Paid via
Tracking no	Notes/return info
Date shipped	Date received

MY PURCHASE

Website/store	Item(s) bought
Order ID	
Order date	Paid via
Tracking no	Notes/return info
Date shipped	Date received

MY PURCHASE

Website/store	Item(s) bought
Order ID	
Order date	Paid via
Tracking no	Notes/return info
Date shipped	Date received

MY PURCHASE

Website/store	Item(s) bought
Order ID	
Order date	Paid via
Tracking no	Notes/return info
Date shipped	Date received

MY PURCHASE

Website/store	Item(s) bought
Order ID	
Order date	Paid via
Tracking no	Notes/return info
Date shipped	Date received

MY PURCHASE

Website/store	Item(s) bought
Order ID	
Order date	Paid via
Tracking no	Notes/return info
Date shipped	Date received

MY PURCHASE

Website/store	Item(s) bought
Order ID	
Order date	Paid via
Tracking no	Notes/return info
Date shipped	Date received

MY PURCHASE

Website/store	Item(s) bought
Order ID	
Order date	Paid via
Tracking no	Notes/return info
Date shipped	Date received

MY PURCHASE

Website/store	Item(s) bought
Order ID	
Order date	Paid via
Tracking no	Notes/return info
Date shipped	Date received

MY PURCHASE

Website/store	Item(s) bought
Order ID	
Order date	Paid via
Tracking no	Notes/return info
Date shipped	Date received

MY PURCHASE

Website/store	Item(s) bought
Order ID	
Order date	Paid via
Tracking no	Notes/return info
Date shipped	Date received

MY PURCHASE

Website/store	Item(s) bought
Order ID	
Order date	Paid via
Tracking no	Notes/return info
Date shipped	Date received

MY PURCHASE

Website/store	Item(s) bought
Order ID	
Order date	Paid via
Tracking no	Notes/return info
Date shipped	Date received

MY PURCHASE

Website/store	Item(s) bought
Order ID	
Order date	Paid via
Tracking no	Notes/return info
Date shipped	Date received

MY PURCHASE

Website/store	Item(s) bought
Order ID	
Order date	Paid via
Tracking no	Notes/return info
Date shipped	Date received

MY PURCHASE

Website/store	Item(s) bought
Order ID	
Order date	Paid via
Tracking no	Notes/return info
Date shipped	Date received

MY PURCHASE

Website/store	Item(s) bought
Order ID	
Order date	Paid via
Tracking no	Notes/return info
Date shipped	Date received

MY PURCHASE

Website/store	Item(s) bought
Order ID	
Order date	Paid via
Tracking no	Notes/return info
Date shipped	Date received

MY PURCHASE

Website/store	Item(s) bought
Order ID	
Order date	Paid via
Tracking no	Notes/return info
Date shipped	Date received

MY PURCHASE

Website/store	Item(s) bought
Order ID	
Order date	Paid via
Tracking no	Notes/return info
Date shipped	Date received

MY PURCHASE

Website/store	Item(s) bought
Order ID	
Order date	Paid via
Tracking no	Notes/return info
Date shipped	Date received

MY PURCHASE

Website/store	Item(s) bought
Order ID	
Order date	Paid via
Tracking no	Notes/return info
Date shipped	Date received

MY PURCHASE

Website/store	Item(s) bought
Order ID	
Order date	Paid via
Tracking no	Notes/return info
Date shipped	Date received

MY PURCHASE

Website/store	Item(s) bought
Order ID	
Order date	Paid via
Tracking no	Notes/return info
Date shipped	Date received

MY PURCHASE

Website/store	Item(s) bought
Order ID	
Order date	Paid via
Tracking no	Notes/return info
Date shipped	Date received

MY PURCHASE

Website/store	Item(s) bought
Order ID	
Order date	Paid via
Tracking no	Notes/return info
Date shipped	Date received

MY PURCHASE

Website/store	Item(s) bought
Order ID	
Order date	Paid via
Tracking no	Notes/return info
Date shipped	Date received

MY PURCHASE

Website/store	Item(s) bought
Order ID	
Order date	Paid via
Tracking no	Notes/return info
Date shipped	Date received

MY PURCHASE

Website/store	Item(s) bought
Order ID	
Order date	Paid via
Tracking no	Notes/return info
Date shipped	Date received

MY PURCHASE

Website/store	Item(s) bought
Order ID	
Order date	Paid via
Tracking no	Notes/return info
Date shipped	Date received

MY PURCHASE

Website/store	Item(s) bought
Order ID	
Order date	Paid via
Tracking no	Notes/return info
Date shipped	Date received

MY PURCHASE

Website/store	Item(s) bought
Order ID	
Order date	Paid via
Tracking no	Notes/return info
Date shipped	Date received

MY PURCHASE

Website/store	Item(s) bought
Order ID	
Order date	Paid via
Tracking no	Notes/return info
Date shipped	Date received

MY PURCHASE

Website/store	Item(s) bought
Order ID	
Order date	Paid via
Tracking no	Notes/return info
Date shipped	Date received

MY PURCHASE

Website/store	Item(s) bought
Order ID	
Order date	Paid via
Tracking no	Notes/return info
Date shipped	Date received

MY PURCHASE

Website/store	Item(s) bought
Order ID	
Order date	Paid via
Tracking no	Notes/return info
Date shipped	Date received

MY PURCHASE

Website/store	Item(s) bought
Order ID	
Order date	Paid via
Tracking no	Notes/return info
Date shipped	Date received

MY PURCHASE

Website/store	Item(s) bought
Order ID	
Order date	Paid via
Tracking no	Notes/return info
Date shipped	Date received

MY PURCHASE

Website/store	Item(s) bought
Order ID	
Order date	Paid via
Tracking no	Notes/return info
Date shipped	Date received

MY PURCHASE

Website/store	Item(s) bought
Order ID	
Order date	Paid via
Tracking no	Notes/return info
Date shipped	Date received

MY PURCHASE

Website/store	Item(s) bought
Order ID	
Order date	Paid via
Tracking no	Notes/return info
Date shipped	Date received

MY PURCHASE

Website/store	Item(s) bought
Order ID	
Order date	Paid via
Tracking no	Notes/return info
Date shipped	Date received

MY PURCHASE

Website/store	Item(s) bought
Order ID	
Order date	Paid via
Tracking no	Notes/return info
Date shipped	Date received

MY PURCHASE

Website/store	Item(s) bought
Order ID	
Order date	Paid via
Tracking no	Notes/return info
Date shipped	Date received

MY PURCHASE

Website/store	Item(s) bought
Order ID	
Order date	Paid via
Tracking no	Notes/return info
Date shipped	Date received

MY PURCHASE

Website/store	Item(s) bought
Order ID	
Order date	Paid via
Tracking no	Notes/return info
Date shipped	Date received

MY PURCHASE

Website/store	Item(s) bought
Order ID	
Order date	Paid via
Tracking no	Notes/return info
Date shipped	Date received

My Purchase

Website/store	Item(s) bought
Order ID	
Order date	Paid via
Tracking no	Notes/return info
Date shipped	Date received

My Purchase

Website/store	Item(s) bought
Order ID	
Order date	Paid via
Tracking no	Notes/return info
Date shipped	Date received

My Purchase

Website/store	Item(s) bought
Order ID	
Order date	Paid via
Tracking no	Notes/return info
Date shipped	Date received

MY PURCHASE

Website/store	Item(s) bought
Order ID	
Order date	Paid via
Tracking no	Notes/return info
Date shipped	Date received

MY PURCHASE

Website/store	Item(s) bought
Order ID	
Order date	Paid via
Tracking no	Notes/return info
Date shipped	Date received

MY PURCHASE

Website/store	Item(s) bought
Order ID	
Order date	Paid via
Tracking no	Notes/return info
Date shipped	Date received

MY PURCHASE

Website/store	Item(s) bought
Order ID	
Order date	Paid via
Tracking no	Notes/return info
Date shipped	Date received

MY PURCHASE

Website/store	Item(s) bought
Order ID	
Order date	Paid via
Tracking no	Notes/return info
Date shipped	Date received

MY PURCHASE

Website/store	Item(s) bought
Order ID	
Order date	Paid via
Tracking no	Notes/return info
Date shipped	Date received

MY PURCHASE

Website/store	Item(s) bought
Order ID	
Order date	Paid via
Tracking no	Notes/return info
Date shipped	Date received

MY PURCHASE

Website/store	Item(s) bought
Order ID	
Order date	Paid via
Tracking no	Notes/return info
Date shipped	Date received

MY PURCHASE

Website/store	Item(s) bought
Order ID	
Order date	Paid via
Tracking no	Notes/return info
Date shipped	Date received

MY PURCHASE

Website/store	Item(s) bought
Order ID	
Order date	Paid via
Tracking no	Notes/return info
Date shipped	Date received

MY PURCHASE

Website/store	Item(s) bought
Order ID	
Order date	Paid via
Tracking no	Notes/return info
Date shipped	Date received

MY PURCHASE

Website/store	Item(s) bought
Order ID	
Order date	Paid via
Tracking no	Notes/return info
Date shipped	Date received

MY PURCHASE

Website/store	Item(s) bought
Order ID	
Order date	Paid via
Tracking no	Notes/return info
Date shipped	Date received

MY PURCHASE

Website/store	Item(s) bought
Order ID	
Order date	Paid via
Tracking no	Notes/return info
Date shipped	Date received

MY PURCHASE

Website/store	Item(s) bought
Order ID	
Order date	Paid via
Tracking no	Notes/return info
Date shipped	Date received

MY PURCHASE

Website/store	Item(s) bought
Order ID	
Order date	Paid via
Tracking no	Notes/return info
Date shipped	Date received

MY PURCHASE

Website/store	Item(s) bought
Order ID	
Order date	Paid via
Tracking no	Notes/return info
Date shipped	Date received

MY PURCHASE

Website/store	Item(s) bought
Order ID	
Order date	Paid via
Tracking no	Notes/return info
Date shipped	Date received

MY PURCHASE

Website/store	Item(s) bought
Order ID	
Order date	Paid via
Tracking no	Notes/return info
Date shipped	Date received

MY PURCHASE

Website/store	Item(s) bought
Order ID	
Order date	Paid via
Tracking no	Notes/return info
Date shipped	Date received

MY PURCHASE

Website/store	Item(s) bought
Order ID	
Order date	Paid via
Tracking no	Notes/return info
Date shipped	Date received

MY PURCHASE

Website/store	Item(s) bought
Order ID	
Order date	Paid via
Tracking no	Notes/return info
Date shipped	Date received

MY PURCHASE

Website/store	Item(s) bought
Order ID	
Order date	Paid via
Tracking no	Notes/return info
Date shipped	Date received

MY PURCHASE

Website/store	Item(s) bought
Order ID	
Order date	Paid via
Tracking no	Notes/return info
Date shipped	Date received

MY PURCHASE

Website/store	Item(s) bought
Order ID	
Order date	Paid via
Tracking no	Notes/return info
Date shipped	Date received

MY PURCHASE

Website/store	Item(s) bought
Order ID	
Order date	Paid via
Tracking no	Notes/return info
Date shipped	Date received

MY PURCHASE

Website/store	Item(s) bought
Order ID	
Order date	Paid via
Tracking no	Notes/return info
Date shipped	Date received

MY PURCHASE

Website/store	Item(s) bought
Order ID	
Order date	Paid via
Tracking no	Notes/return info
Date shipped	Date received

MY PURCHASE

Website/store	Item(s) bought
Order ID	
Order date	Paid via
Tracking no	Notes/return info
Date shipped	Date received

MY PURCHASE

Website/store	Item(s) bought
Order ID	
Order date	Paid via
Tracking no	Notes/return info
Date shipped	Date received

MY PURCHASE

Website/store	Item(s) bought
Order ID	
Order date	Paid via
Tracking no	Notes/return info
Date shipped	Date received

MY PURCHASE

Website/store	Item(s) bought
Order ID	
Order date	Paid via
Tracking no	Notes/return info
Date shipped	Date received

MY PURCHASE

Website/store	Item(s) bought
Order ID	
Order date	Paid via
Tracking no	Notes/return info
Date shipped	Date received

MY PURCHASE

Website/store	Item(s) bought
Order ID	
Order date	Paid via
Tracking no	Notes/return info
Date shipped	Date received

MY PURCHASE

Website/store	Item(s) bought
Order ID	
Order date	Paid via
Tracking no	Notes/return info
Date shipped	Date received

MY PURCHASE

Website/store	Item(s) bought
Order ID	
Order date	Paid via
Tracking no	Notes/return info
Date shipped	Date received

MY PURCHASE

Website/store	Item(s) bought
Order ID	
Order date	Paid via
Tracking no	Notes/return info
Date shipped	Date received

MY PURCHASE

Website/store	Item(s) bought
Order ID	
Order date	Paid via
Tracking no	Notes/return info
Date shipped	Date received

MY PURCHASE

Website/store	Item(s) bought
Order ID	
Order date	Paid via
Tracking no	Notes/return info
Date shipped	Date received

MY PURCHASE

Website/store	Item(s) bought
Order ID	
Order date	Paid via
Tracking no	Notes/return info
Date shipped	Date received

MY PURCHASE

Website/store	Item(s) bought
Order ID	
Order date	Paid via
Tracking no	Notes/return info
Date shipped	Date received

MY PURCHASE

Website/store	Item(s) bought
Order ID	
Order date	Paid via
Tracking no	Notes/return info
Date shipped	Date received

MY PURCHASE

Website/store	Item(s) bought
Order ID	
Order date	Paid via
Tracking no	Notes/return info
Date shipped	Date received

MY PURCHASE

Website/store	Item(s) bought
Order ID	
Order date	Paid via
Tracking no	Notes/return info
Date shipped	Date received

MY PURCHASE

Website/store	Item(s) bought
Order ID	
Order date	Paid via
Tracking no	Notes/return info
Date shipped	Date received

MY PURCHASE

Website/store	Item(s) bought
Order ID	
Order date	Paid via
Tracking no	Notes/return info
Date shipped	Date received

MY PURCHASE

Website/store	Item(s) bought
Order ID	
Order date	Paid via
Tracking no	Notes/return info
Date shipped	Date received

MY PURCHASE

Website/store	Item(s) bought
Order ID	
Order date	Paid via
Tracking no	Notes/return info
Date shipped	Date received

MY PURCHASE

Website/store	Item(s) bought
Order ID	
Order date	Paid via
Tracking no	Notes/return info
Date shipped	Date received

MY PURCHASE

Website/store	Item(s) bought
Order ID	
Order date	Paid via
Tracking no	Notes/return info
Date shipped	Date received

MY PURCHASE

Website/store	Item(s) bought
Order ID	
Order date	Paid via
Tracking no	Notes/return info
Date shipped	Date received

MY PURCHASE

Website/store	Item(s) bought
Order ID	
Order date	Paid via
Tracking no	Notes/return info
Date shipped	Date received

MY PURCHASE

Website/store	Item(s) bought
Order ID	
Order date	Paid via
Tracking no	Notes/return info
Date shipped	Date received

MY PURCHASE

Website/store	Item(s) bought
Order ID	
Order date	Paid via
Tracking no	Notes/return info
Date shipped	Date received

MY PURCHASE

Website/store	Item(s) bought
Order ID	
Order date	Paid via
Tracking no	Notes/return info
Date shipped	Date received

MY PURCHASE

Website/store	Item(s) bought
Order ID	
Order date	Paid via
Tracking no	Notes/return info
Date shipped	Date received

MY PURCHASE

Website/store	Item(s) bought
Order ID	
Order date	Paid via
Tracking no	Notes/return info
Date shipped	Date received

My Purchase

Website/store	Item(s) bought
Order ID	
Order date	Paid via
Tracking no	Notes/return info
Date shipped	Date received

My Purchase

Website/store	Item(s) bought
Order ID	
Order date	Paid via
Tracking no	Notes/return info
Date shipped	Date received

My Purchase

Website/store	Item(s) bought
Order ID	
Order date	Paid via
Tracking no	Notes/return info
Date shipped	Date received

MY PURCHASE

Website/store	Item(s) bought
Order ID	
Order date	Paid via
Tracking no	Notes/return info
Date shipped	Date received

MY PURCHASE

Website/store	Item(s) bought
Order ID	
Order date	Paid via
Tracking no	Notes/return info
Date shipped	Date received

MY PURCHASE

Website/store	Item(s) bought
Order ID	
Order date	Paid via
Tracking no	Notes/return info
Date shipped	Date received

MY PURCHASE

Website/store	Item(s) bought
Order ID	
Order date	Paid via
Tracking no	Notes/return info
Date shipped	Date received

MY PURCHASE

Website/store	Item(s) bought
Order ID	
Order date	Paid via
Tracking no	Notes/return info
Date shipped	Date received

MY PURCHASE

Website/store	Item(s) bought
Order ID	
Order date	Paid via
Tracking no	Notes/return info
Date shipped	Date received

MY PURCHASE

Website/store	Item(s) bought
Order ID	
Order date	Paid via
Tracking no	Notes/return info
Date shipped	Date received

MY PURCHASE

Website/store	Item(s) bought
Order ID	
Order date	Paid via
Tracking no	Notes/return info
Date shipped	Date received

MY PURCHASE

Website/store	Item(s) bought
Order ID	
Order date	Paid via
Tracking no	Notes/return info
Date shipped	Date received

Made in the USA
Las Vegas, NV
20 December 2024

14951888R00069